KU-072-065

KINGFISHER
An imprint of Kingfisher Publications Plc
New Penderel House
283-288 High Holborn
London WC1V 7HZ
www.kingfisherpub.com

First published by Kingfisher 2004
2 4 6 8 10 9 7 5 3 1

This selection copyright © Kingfisher Publications Plc 1984
Illustrations copyright © Mik Brown 1984, 1987, 1994
Cover illustration copyright © Tony Trimmer 2004

The moral rights of the illustrators have been asserted.

All rights reserved. No part of this publication may be
reproduced, stored in a retrieval system or transmitted by
any means electronic, mechanical, photocopying or
otherwise, without the prior permission of the publisher.

A CIP catalogue record for this book is
available from the British Library.

ISBN 978-0-7534-0985-5

Printed in India
TS/THOM/HBM(PICA)/90SHES/F

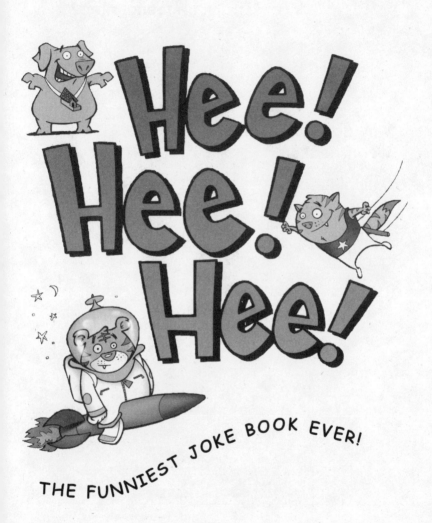

Hee! Hee! Hee!

THE FUNNIEST JOKE BOOK EVER!

KINGFISHER

Why did the elephant paint his toenails red?

So he could hide in the cherry tree.

Why does an elephant wear sneakers?

So that he can sneak up on mice.

What time is it when an elephant sits on the fence?

Time to fix the fence.

4

How do you know when there's an elephant under your bed?

When your nose touches the ceiling.

What's the difference between an elephant and a flea?

An elephant can have fleas, but a flea can't have elephants.

Why were the elephants thrown out of the swimming-pool?

Because they couldn't hold their trunks up.

How do you know when there's an elephant in the refrigerator?

When you can't shut the door.

THUD!

What do you get if you cross an elephant with a kangaroo?

Great big holes all over Australia.

6

What do you call an elephant that flies?

A jumbo jet.

**Why did the elephant paint
himself different colours?**

Because he wanted
to hide in the crayon box.

**How does an elephant
get down from a tree?**

He sits on a leaf and
waits for autumn.

What did the elephant say to the orange?

Let's play squash.

Why are elephants so wrinkled?

Have you ever tried ironing one?

One snake said to another:

"Are we supposed to be poisonous?"
"Why?"
"Because I've just bitten my lip."

What do you get if you cross a snake with a magician?

Abra da cobra.

What's green and slimy and goes *hith*?

A snake with a lisp.

**What do polar bears
have for lunch?**

Ice burgers.

**What gets wet
as it dries?**

A towel.

**What animal do you look
like in the bath?**

A little
bear.

What's white outside, green inside and hops?

A frog sandwich.

Where do tadpoles turn into frogs?

In the croakroom.

FREDA: "Will I be able to read with these glasses?"

FRED: "You certainly will."

FREDA: "That's good. I couldn't before."

Where do you take a frog with bad eyesight?

To the hoptician.

What's red and flies and wobbles at the same time?

A jellycopter.

What's green and can jump a mile a minute?

A frog with hiccups.

**What's scaly,
has a hard shell
and bounces?**

A tortoise on a
pogo-stick.

BOING!
BOING!

**What's black and shiny,
lives in trees and is
very dangerous?**

A crow with a machine-gun.

**What was the tortoise doing
on the motorway?**

About 150 millimetres an hour.

A giraffe, an elephant, a camel, a bear, a pig and a frog, two mice and a snake all sheltered under one umbrella; how many got wet?

None, it wasn't raining.

Why are goldfish red?

The water makes them rusty.

What did the sardine call the submarine?

A can of people.

TEACHER: "You should have been here at 9 o'clock."

PUPIL: "Why, what happened?"

What kind of noise annoys an oyster?

A noisy noise annoys an oyster.

What's yellow and highly dangerous?

Shark-infested custard.

What do you get from a bad-tempered shark?

As far away as possible.

What do you call someone with a seagull on his head?

Cliff.

What do you get if you cross a snowman with a tiger?

Frostbite.

GRRRR!

What's yellow and black with red spots?

A leopard with measles.

LION: "You're a cheater!"

CHEETAH: "You're lion!"

Why is it hard for leopards to hide?

Because they're always spotted.

I CAN SEE YOU!

If athletes get athlete's foot, what do astronauts get?

Missile-toe.

What do astronauts eat for lunch?

Launch-meat sandwiches.

What do you call a mad astronaut?

An astronut.

How do you get a baby astronaut to sleep?

You rock-et.

SPLOP!

What did the astronaut see in his frying pan?

An unidentified frying object.

What do you give a sick pig?

Oinkment.

What kind of tie does a pig wear?

A pig-sty.

Why is getting up in the morning like a pig's tail?

Because it's twirly (too early).

One camel said to another:

"Did you know the cleverest camel in
   the desert was deaf?"
"Really — who is it?"
"Pardon?"

**What was the name of
the camel without a hump?**

Humphrey.

**What animal with two humps
can be found at
the North Pole?**

A lost camel.

23

"Waiter, this soup tastes funny."

"Then why aren't you laughing?"

"Waiter, what's this fly doing in my soup?"

"Looks like it's learning to swim, sir."

"Waiter, there's a small slug on this lettuce."

"Sorry, sir, shall I get you a bigger one?"

"Waiter, there's a mouse in my hamburger."

"Don't shout, sir, or everyone will want one."

"Waiter, do you have frogs' legs?"

"No, sir, I've always walked like this."

"Waiter, there's a caterpillar on my salad."

"Don't worry, sir, there's no extra charge."

"Waiter, there's a fly in my soup."

"Don't worry, sir, that spider on your bread will soon get rid of it."

"Waiter, your thumb is in my soup."

"That's okay, madam, it's not hot."

"Waiter, this coffee is terrible — it tastes like earth!"

"Yes, sir, it was ground yesterday."

"Waiter, is there soup on the menu?"

"No, madam, I wiped it off."

"Waiter, this egg is bad."

"Don't blame me, madam, I only laid the table."

"Waiter, bring me something to eat, and make it snappy."

"How about a crocodile sandwich, sir."

What did the pony say when he coughed?

"Excuse me, I'm just a little horse."

What did the hungry donkey say when it had only thistles to eat?

"Thist-le have to do."

Who always goes to bed with shoes on?

A horse.

How do you start a flea race?

1, 2, flea, go.

What did the earwig say when it fell off the cliff?

"'Ere we go."

What lies down a hundred feet in the air?

A centipede.

What bee can never be understood?

A mumble-bee.

Why do bees hum?

Because they don't know the words.

What is the biggest ant?

An elephant.

How can you tell which end of a worm is which?

Tickle its middle and see which end smiles.

When did the fly fly?

When the spider spied her.

When the dentist put his fingers in the crocodile's mouth to see how many teeth it had, what did the crocodile do?

It closed its mouth to see how many fingers the dentist had.

What's a crocodile's favourite card game?

Snap.

What do you call a sick crocodile?

An illigator.

**What's the difference
between a crocodile
and a postbox?**

If you don't know, watch out
when you next post a letter.

**Have you heard
the joke about
the watermelon?**

It's pitiful.

**What's green and
dangerous and
good at arithmetic?**

A crocodile
with a
calculator.

How do you tell a rabbit from a gorilla?

A rabbit doesn't look like a gorilla.

What is a twip?

A twip is what a wabbit makes when he wides a twain.

What do you get if you pour hot water down a rabbit-hole?

Hot-cross bunnies.

34

"If I give you three rabbits . . .

. . . and then I give you two rabbits . .

. . . how many rabbits will you have?"

"Six."   "Six?"

"Yes, I've got one already."

How do you stop a skunk from smelling?

Hold its nose.

**What do you get
if you cross a
bear with a skunk?**

Winnie the Pooh.

**What do skunks have that no
other animals have?**

Baby skunks.

What's black and white and very noisy?

A skunk with a drum kit.

What's black and white and has sixteen wheels?

A zebra on roller skates.

What do you call a gorilla wearing headphones?

Anything, he can't hear you.

Why does a monkey scratch himself?

Because he's the only one who knows where it itches.

How do you catch a monkey?

Hang upside down in a tree and make a noise like a banana.

Why are monsters forgetful?

Because everything you tell them goes in one ear and out the others.

Why did the monster knit herself three socks?

Because she grew another foot.

What's the difference between a huge, ugly, smelly monster and a sweet?

People like sweets.

"What has a purple-spotted body, ten hairy legs and big eyes on stalks?"

"I don't know, but there's one crawling up your leg."

What do you say when you meet a two-headed monster?

"Hello, hello!"

What is the best way to speak to a monster?

From a long distance.

What's big, red and prickly, has three eyes and eats rocks?

A big, red, prickly, three-eyed rock-eater.

How does a monster count to fifteen?

On its fingers.

"Doctor, doctor, I feel like a bell."

"Take these and, if they don't work, give me a ring."

"Doctor, doctor, I keep thinking I'm a dustbin."

"Don't talk rubbish."

"Doctor, doctor, I keep forgetting things."

"When did this start happening?"

"When did what start happening?"

Why didn't the skeleton go to the party?

It had no body to go with.

"Doctor, doctor, I can't sleep at night."

"Sleep on the wardrobe and you'll soon drop off."

DOCTOR: "Did you drink your orange juice after your bath?"

PATIENT: "After drinking the bath, I didn't have much room for the orange juice."

"Doctor, doctor, my hair keeps falling out. Can you give me something to keep it in?"

"How about a paper bag?"

"Doctor, doctor, I feel like an apple."

"Come over here, I won't bite you."

Doctor, doctor, I keep thinking I'm invisible."

"Who said that?"

**"Doctor, doctor, I feel like
a pair of curtains."**

"Pull yourself together."

"Doctor, doctor, I've got a terrible sore throat."

"Go over to the window and stick your
tongue out."

"Will that help my throat?"

"No, I just don't like the man next door."

**"Doctor, doctor,
everybody
ignores me."**

"Next, please."

**"If I had eight hedgehogs in one hand
and seven hedgehogs in the other,
what would I have?"**

"Big hands."

**Why did the hedgehog
wear red boots?**

Because his brown ones
were at the mender's.

What did the hedgehog say to the cactus?

"Is that you, Mama?"

Where would you find a prehistoric cow?

In a moo-seum.

What do you get if you cross a cow, a sheep and a goat?

The Milky Baa Kid.

Which cows have the shortest legs?

The smallest ones.

Why did the cow go over the hill?

Because it couldn't go under it.

Where do cows go on a Saturday night?

To the moo-vies.

What goes OOM OOM?

A cow walking backwards.

What do you call a bull asleep on the ground?

A bulldozer.

FIRST COW: "Moo"

SECOND COW: "Baa-a-a."

FIRST COW: "What do you mean 'Baa-a-a'?"

SECOND COW: "I'm learning a foreign language."

MOOO!

BAAA!

HOW NOW BROWN SHEEP.

**What's white,
has four legs
and a trunk?**

A mouse going
on holiday.

**What do angry mice send each other
at Christmas?**

Cross-mouse cards.

**What's brown,
has four legs
and a trunk?**

A mouse coming
back from holiday.

What do mice do in the daytime?

Mousework.

How can you tell one cat from another?

Look them up in a catalogue.

What's grey, has four legs and weighs one-and-a-half pounds?

A fat mouse.

What has the head of a cat, the tail of a cat, but is not a cat?

A kitten.

What works in a circus, does somersaults and meows?

An acrocat.

There are ten copycats in a car, one gets out, how many are left?

None.

Why do cats have furry coats?

Because they'd look silly in plastic macs.

Spell "mousetrap" in three letters.

C-A-T.

How do you stop your dog barking in the hall?

Put it outside.

"Your dog's been chasing a man on a bicycle."

"Don't be silly! My dog can't ride a bicycle."

Tic! Toc!

What goes tick-tock, bow-wow, tick-tock, bow-wow?

A watch-dog.

What did the puppy say when it sat on sandpaper?

"Ruff!"

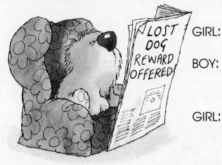

GIRL: "I've lost my dog."

BOY: "Why don't you put an ad in the paper?"

GIRL: "Don't be silly! My dog can't read."

Why does a dog wag its tail?

Because no one will wag it for him.

How does a sparrow with engine trouble manage to land safely?

With its sparrowchute.

What do you get if you cross a chicken with a cement mixer?

A brick-layer.

What's black and white and red all over?

A sunburnt penguin.

GIRL: "I've found a penguin."

BOY: "Why don't you take it to the zoo?"

GIRL: "I took it to the zoo yesterday.
Today we're going to the cinema."

**Why don't ducks tell jokes
when they're flying?**

Because they would
quack up.

**Why do birds fly south
in the winter?**

Because it's too
far to walk.

56

What do you get if you cross a parrot with an alligator?

Something that bites your hand off and says, "Who's a pretty boy then?"

WHO'S A PRETTY BOY THEN?

What do you call a crate of ducks?

A box of quackers.

"Mummy, mummy, I've just swallowed my mouth organ!"

"Just be glad you don't play the piano."

GULP!

Why did the mother kangaroo scold her baby?

Because he'd been eating biscuits in bed.

JIM: "What's the matter?"

TOM: "My new shoes hurt."

JIM: "That's because you've got them on the wrong feet."

TOM: "Well, they're the only feet I have."

What does an angry kangaroo do?

Get hopping mad.

SON: "Can I have another glass of water?"

FATHER: "Another? This will be your tenth!"

SON: "I know, but my room's on fire."

What do you get if you cross a kangaroo with a sheep?

A woolly jumper.

Where do you find hippos?

It depends where you left them.

Which animal is always laughing.

A happy-potamus.

How do you tell the difference between a hippo and a banana?

If it's a hippo, you can't pick it up.

What does a hippo have if its head is hot, one foot is cold and it sees spots?

A polka-dotted sock over its head.

Where did Napoleon keep his armies?

Up his sleevies.

What pet makes the loudest noise?

A trumpet.

Where did Humpty Dumpty leave his hat?

Humpty dumped his hat on the wall.

What has two arms, two wings, two tails, three heads, three bodies and eight legs?

A man on a horse holding a chicken.

Other titles in the *Sidesplitters* series for you to enjoy:

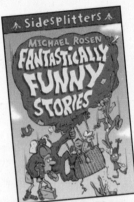

Michael Rosen
FANTASTICALLY FUNNY STORIES

HA! HA! HA!

Over 350 very funny jokes

Hee! Hee! Hee!

THE FUNNIEST JOKE BOOK EVER!

HO HO HO!

150 CRACKING CHRISTMAS JOKES

KNOCK KNOCK!

The Best Knock Knock Jokes Ever!

Seriously Silly School Jokes

UNFORGETTABLE ELEPHANT JOKES

WHAT A HOOT!

OVER 150 HiLarious ANiMaL JOKES

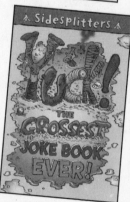

UK!
THE GROSSEST JOKE BOOK EVER!